Billy Taylor
PIANO STYLES

Front cover photo by William "PoPsie" Randolph
www.PoPsiePhotos.com

Back cover photo by Jimmy Katz

ISBN 13: 978-1-4234-1226-7
ISBN 10: 1-4234-1226-5

HAL•LEONARD®
CORPORATION
7777 W. BLUEMOUND RD. P.O. BOX 13819 MILWAUKEE, WI 53213

In Australia Contact:
Hal Leonard Australia Pty. Ltd.
4 Lentara Court
Cheltenham, Victoria, 3192 Australia
Email: ausadmin@halleonard.com

Visit Hal Leonard Online at
www.halleonard.com

CONTENTS

BE-BOP

WHAT IS BE-BOP?

The most truly American music is jazz, an art form originated and used as a medium of expression by African-Americans. Jazz has undergone many changes and developments since it came into being near the end of the 19th century. One revolutionary development is called "Be-Bop."

Be-Bop is the result of several years of experimentation—individually and collectively—by a group of progressive young jazz musicians. Not content to play in the same stereotyped fashion that had reached its zenith around 1936, these imaginative and talented musicians enlarged the scope of jazz rhythmically, melodically, and harmonically, radically changing its sound with their unusual use of intervals, passing notes, rubato, and other devices that we shall discuss in more detail later.

Be-Bop, like all other forms of jazz, owes much of its development to improvisation and the ingenuity of the musicians who use it as their medium of expression. Improvisation is an essential part of Be-Bop because it is the only way these musicians can express the essence of a given musical composition in an unrestricted yet creative manner.

The basis of Be-Bop improvisation is the alteration (or revision) of the composition being played and the development of its rhythmic, harmonic, and melodic potentials according to the mood and conception of the player. However, the feeling of spontaneity is the same whether the performer is creating an original composition based on the thematic structure of a popular song, or re-creating a sequence of melodic, harmonic, or rhythmic ideas originally conceived by a fellow Be-Bop musician.

Because of the frequent use in Be-Bop of rubato, double-time, polyrhythms, and unusual accents, it is sometimes difficult to maintain a beat that has a relaxed and natural swing. However, no matter how syncopated or intricate a Be-Bop passage may be, the beat must never lose its vitality. It must swing or it is not good Be-Bop. One of the most distinguishing features of good jazz playing is that it is basically a form of creative expression against the limitation of a steady beat. This steady beat may be actually played (as in the older forms of jazz) or merely suggested (as it often is in Be-Bop); but no matter how it is indicated, it must be felt to such an extent that it always retains its validity.

Before one can hope to play Be-Bop, one must have a clear aural impression of it. The best way to develop a conception of this style is to hear it played by its leading exponents. Hear them—both in person and on recordings—if you can. Listen not only to the piano, but also to all of the instruments, as they play separately and in ensemble. Analyze their efforts carefully and try to grasp the motivating spirit of the music. Then, when at last you feel its nuances and subtleties, try to create original ideas in this idiom based on your own musical experience.

Some excellent examples of Be-Bop piano playing and the principles advocated in this book may be found in the recorded performances of Bud Powell, Hank Jones, Al Haig, Mary Lou Williams, George Shearing, and Billy Taylor.

RHYTHM

The basic components of rhythm are:
1. Pulse (or beat): the regular recurrence of time distances.
2. Accent: the division of pulse into units or measures (i.e., 2/4, 3/4, 4/4, etc.).

Example 1

3. Long and short time values (duration of notes).
4. Musical figures or ideas.
5. Phrases and the balancing of phrases.

The smallest unit expressing the fundamental beat of a composition is the measure. Be-Bop is played and written in 4/4 meter; that is, four beats in each measure. Though at times these beats may be silent or highly subdivided, the feeling of four beats to a measure must prevail. This feeling of four beats to a measure is one of the most distinguishing features of the "Be-Bop beat."

Example 2

Example 3

While the Be-Bop beat must be precise rhythmically, it must also be musical and relaxed, not mechanical. If the player keeps this in mind, the music will have more continuity and authority.

The true function of syncopation is to enhance the power of the beat. The best Be-Bop musicians practice this avidly. However, their relaxed conception of syncopation is based on a feeling for the beat that is so strong that it makes each phrase swing. This beat-background is like the canvas to the artist, a time surface on which musical designs may be developed.

In the following example, note how at the end of the first bar the sound starts at the same time with both hands and also ceases at the same time in bar 2, despite the fact that the right hand has two sets of sounds and the left hand only one.

Example 4

As may be seen in Example 5, the effect of the syncopation is enhanced by the use of accents, articulation, and careful observation of the duration of each note and each rest.

In order to give more expression to certain notes without giving them undue tonal emphasis, it is sometimes desirable to change the relative time values. This impromptu lengthening of one note and shortening of another is really rubato. If some notes mean more to the player than others, he is inclined to dwell upon them; but when he is limited by the jazz beat, he must compensate for this by giving less time to the others so that "it comes out even in the end." Remember, it is the time value of the notes which is altered, not the total time value of the phrases; above all, the beat must not fluctuate.

Example 5

Example 6

Example 7

Example 8

Polyrhythm, or the playing of several rhythms simultaneously, is another device often used in playing Be-Bop. Example 9 demonstrates groups of threes played against the steady 4/4 beat.

Example 9

The following type of polyrhythmic figure is sometimes used when playing with a group. The "walking" bass indicates the basic beat, while the rest of the rhythm section may either accent the triplets along with the piano, or play different rhythmic figures of their own.

If you tap your foot in time with the bass rhythm and play the piano part at the same time, you will be demonstrating how each rhythmic line is leading a life of its own.

Example 10

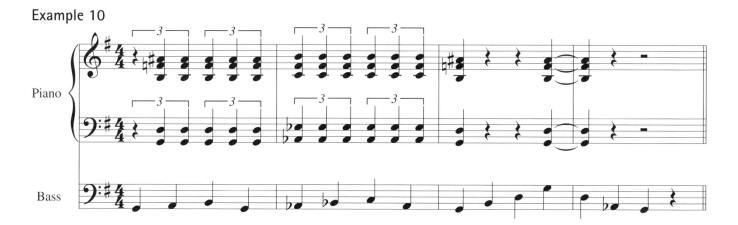

MELODY

A melody is a series of single tones, rhythmically arranged so as to produce a pleasing effect on the ear. Be-Bop melodies have been harshly criticized on many occasions because listeners found that their ears were affected in a manner far from pleasant by the unusual intervals, which occur so frequently.

However, a good Be-Bop melody can be very pleasing to hear if one understands the manner in which the tones comprising its phrases are related.

In general, the tones that comprise Be-Bop phrases are related harmonically. The phrases may consist of a few notes, or they may be several measures long. This depends entirely on the ingenuity or disposition of the performer or composer. An illustration of this harmonic relationship is taken from an original Be-Bop tune, "B.T.'s-D.T.'s." The melody itself suggests the harmony of the piece.

Example 11: B.T.'s–D.T.'s (excerpt)

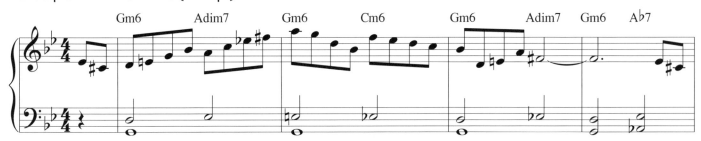

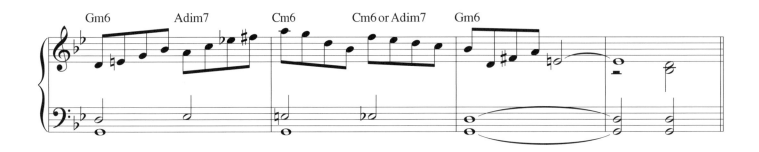

The upper and lower neighbor notes may be placed before their principle tone (in either order) as passing tones. This is called a double appoggiatura and is found frequently in Be-Bop melodies.

Active tones create a tension, which is not relieved until rest tones are reached. However, due to the fact that in many instances these active tones are not resolved at once (sometimes they are not resolved at all), anyone wishing to play Be-Bop must become very familiar with the way they sound before and after resolution. Once the ear is conditioned and attuned to the sound of the flatted fifth, the major and minor seventh, the raised and lowered ninth, etc. (see Ex. 14), it becomes easier to hear the relationship of notes that might otherwise sound wrong. This point cannot be stressed too much because Be-Bop melodies often employ skips of wide and sometimes unexpected intervals. It is a common practice to end a phrase (or a tune) on a tone that is commonly thought of as an active tone.

Example 12 ends on the unresolved major seventh of the D♭ chord.

Example 12

Careful fingering will facilitate the playing of the following piece. Use the fingering that best fits your hand, especially in the bridge of the first chorus.

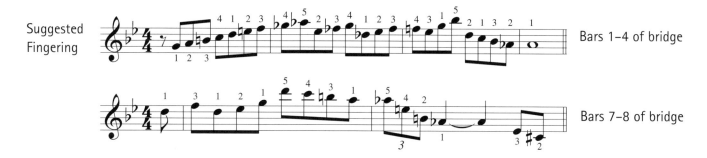

Suggested Fingering — Bars 1–4 of bridge

Bars 7–8 of bridge

Though the tempo is indicated as fast, it should be played in a relaxed manner, always keeping a steady beat.

B.T.'S – D.T.'S

by BILLY TAYLOR

Note how the melody in Example 13 skips up in fourths, then down in fourths, in bar 1. The F♯ (raised 11th of the C chord) is used as a passing tone to G (9th of the F chord) in bar 2. The melody skips down to C (an interval of a fifth) then moves upward, first in whole steps, then chromatically to G (the 13th of the B♭ chord). It then descends scalewise from E♭ to C in bar 3. Skipping a minor third to A natural and then down a perfect fifth from B♭ to E♭, it uses E natural as a passing tone and ends on G (the major 7th of the A♭ chord).

Example 13

Embellishments

Three types of ornamental notes are found frequently in Be-Bop. They are:

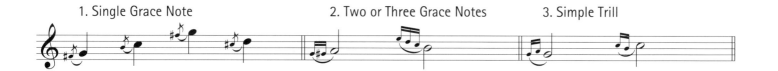

When used with discretion these embellishments greatly increase the feeling of spontaneity in Be-Bop melodies.

HARMONY

One of the most important innovations made by the creators of Be-Bop is the incorporation of modern harmonic principles into their idiom. Their fondness for dissonance and their extensive use of altered chords, various types of seventh chords, and their extensions into ninths, elevenths, and thirteenths has done much to expand the potentials of jazz.

The chords most frequently used when playing Be-Bop on the piano are given below: "Large" means the seventh is major, and "small" indicates a minor seventh.

Example 14

Example 15

Invert these chords and play them in all keys; then you will have a working knowledge of the

For playing with groups and for special solo effects, the locked hand style (so called because both hands move in the same direction simultaneously) is often employed by Be-Bop pianists.

Example 16

The top note (or melody note) doubles the bass.

Example 17

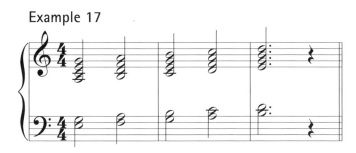

The two highest notes double the two lowest notes.

Here is an illustration of the locked hand style taken from an improvisation by Billy Taylor.

Example 18

In the search for new sounds in jazz, polytonal (or polyharmonic) effects are often achieved. One of the most effective ways of doing this is to superimpose one chord upon another. The sounds that are produced as a result of this type of experimentation are often used very effectively by many of the more imaginative modern jazz pianists.

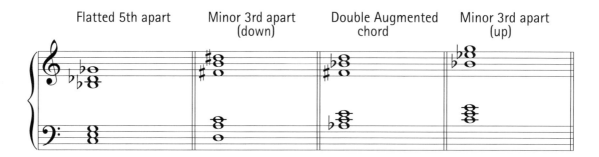

IMPROVISATION

In order to illustrate Be-Bop improvisation and how it may be practiced on a familiar tune, let us take the old Scotch air "Loch Lomond."

Example 19: Loch Lomond

Traditional

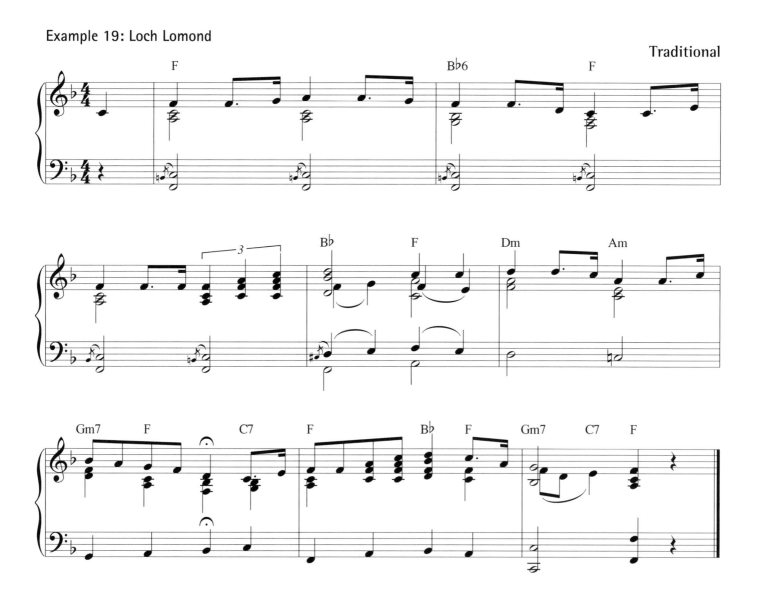

As our first step toward improvisation, let us revise the harmony using some of the chords shown previously.

Example 20

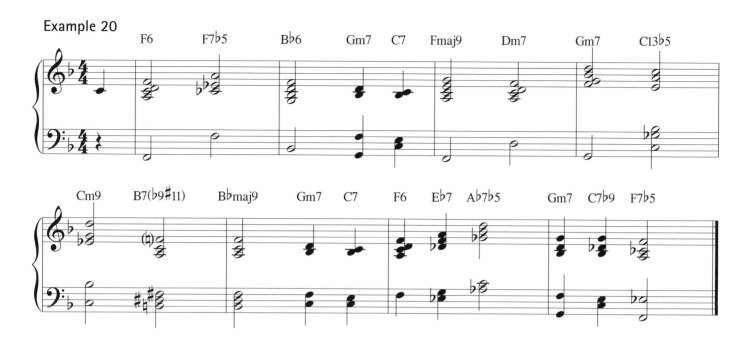

Now let us change the phrasing of the melody from academic to Be-Bop.

Example 21

In the older forms of jazz, the bass was often played like this:

Example 22

In Be-Bop some of these forms may be used for certain effects, but for the most part the bass emphasizes the harmonic patterns.

With the preceding illustrations in mind, let us put our revised melody and harmony of "Loch Lomond" together.

Example 23

Now our final step: the creation of a new melody based on our revision of the academic harmonization of the tune.

Example 24

We now have a new composition, since neither the melody, harmony, nor rhythm is the same as that of "Loch Lomond." So, in honor of its origin we will call our "new" composition "Scotticism."

Here's a tune expressing admiration for Be-Bop pioneer Charlie "Bird" Parker.

BIRDWATCHER

by BILLY TAYLOR

Medium Bop groove

One of the special areas of development in Be-Bop was Latin jazz. Dizzy Gillespie updated the "Spanish tinge" often found in the work of Jelly Roll Morton, Duke Ellington, and musicians of other periods by utilizing an Afro-Cuban rhythmic pulse in many of his compositions and arrangements ("Manteca," "Algo Buena," "Night in Tunisia," etc.). He did not merely perform with Latin rhythm sections like Machito; he worked off both rhythmic sources in the same way that a bi-lingual person uses two languages with equal facility.

When I was house pianist at Birdland I taught "Titoro" to Dizzy Gillespie and he played it often in concert with his small groups. Both "Titoro" and "Mambomania" are representative of the kinds of Latin jazz Gillespie and other Be-Bop musicians improvised on.

TITORO

by BILLY TAYLOR

MAMBOMANIA

by BILLY TAYLOR

To Coda

D.S. al Coda

CODA

In this next tune, play the bass figure evenly and keep the beat as steady as possible. It is simply 1-2-3-4, starting a half beat ahead of the bar. The piece should be played without pedal. In the 14th bar before the end, be sure to play both 8th and quarter triplets evenly.

GOOD GROOVE

by BILLY TAYLOR

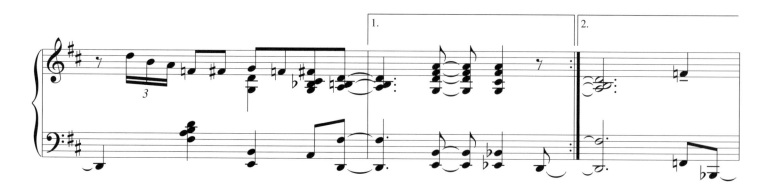

27

SOUNDS IN THE NIGHT

by BILLY TAYLOR

Rubato

D.S. al Fine

Familiarize yourself with this original Be-Bop tune; then improvise on it, using active tones to
lengthen your phrases and give them continuity. Keep your beat steady and relaxed.

DECLIVITY

by BILLY TAYLOR

Here is a Be-Bop arrangement of the old favorite "Good Night Ladies." Analyze it and then try out your own ideas on this theme. Remember: keep the beat relaxed no matter what you play in your improvisation.

GOOD NIGHT LADIES

by BILLY TAYLOR

BOOGIE-WOOGIE

WHAT IS BOOGIE-WOOGIE?

Boogie-Woogie is a style of jazz piano playing that dates back to the early 1900s. Its most characteristic feature is the use of recurring bass patterns that lay the foundation, rhythmically and harmonically, for the sometimes short but always rhythmic melodic passages. The repetition of these bass patterns gives Boogie-Woogie its unique drive and is the reason that it is often called "eight to the bar." This is actually a misnomer because Boogie-Woogie is usually written in 4/4 time. The four beats may either be stated as four quarter notes or subdivided in many ways—resulting in more or fewer than eight notes to a measure, depending on the type of bass pattern used.

No one knows exactly where it was originated or by whom, but jazz pioneers like Jelly Roll Morton and old time pianists like Richard M. Jones recall hearing Boogie-Woogie played by illiterate wandering musicians when they were children. Morton says that in those days it was called "Honky-Tonk" music, and was played for the most part by second-rate jazz pianists. Like many other early jazz styles it was taken from the South to Chicago, where in the hands of men like Jim Yancey it became very popular. However, it was soon replaced by other less percussive styles of piano playing, and it was not until the middle 1930s that it was rediscovered by John Hammond and brought to New York where it quickly received new and more lasting fame. Its foremost exponents at this time were the sensational Albert Ammons, Pete Johnson, and Meade "Lux" Lewis.

The Boogie-Woogie of today has not changed much from the Boogie-Woogie of the Ragtime era. New harmonies and different melodies have been added, but it still derives its unique drive from the same type of repeated bass pattern that first distinguished it from other jazz piano styles. Its beat is still unmistakable and even though much of its appeal is based on the psychology of repetition, the contagious development of musical ideas present in all jazz styles is very much in evidence when one improvises in this style. In its present form, Boogie-Woogie is one of the most rhythmic and exciting styles of jazz piano playing.

There are many excellent recorded examples of pianists playing in this exciting manner, and the importance of listening to performances (in person or on recordings) by artists like Ammons, Johnson, and Lewis cannot be stressed too much. Boogie-Woogie must swing, and as in other jazz piano styles, passages that are not improvised must have the same feeling of spontaneity that characterizes the robust and colorful extemporizations of its best exponents.

THE BOOGIE BEAT

Boogie-Woogie is written in 4/4 time and the basic four beats in each measure may be stated as four quarter notes:

Example 1

Or subdivided in many ways:

Example 2

Example 4

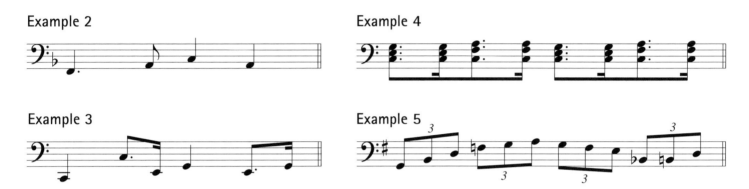

Example 3

Example 5

The function of the Boogie-Woogie bass line is twofold. It establishes and maintains the basic beat of the piece and at the same time forms a harmonic background for whatever is being played with the right hand. Therefore, many Boogie-Woogie bass patterns are constructed by using the tones of the basic chords.

Example 6

Tones of the tonic chord with neighboring notes:

Example 7

Tones of the tonic chord with passing notes:

Example 8

Or sometimes just the basic chords alone:

Example 9

Here are a few of the most popular Boogie-Woogie bass patterns:

Example 10

HARMONY

A vast majority of Boogie-Woogie pieces are based on the harmonic structure of the twelve-bar blues. This structure consists of three basic chords.

Example 11

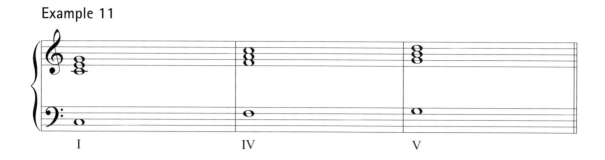

    I   IV   V

The traditional Boogie-Woogie blues sequence is easy to memorize, so play it in the key of C and then transpose it to other keys

Example 12

There are of course many secondary chords that may be added to this sequence, but that is left to the individual performer. As a general rule the harmonies in Boogie-Woogie piano playing are relatively simple. However, tonal clusters are frequently used in the right hand.

Example 13

Harmonic liberties are frequently taken.

Example 14

In later examples you will note the use of embellishments, chromatic tones, and passing tones, as well as the tonal clusters and harmonic liberties just mentioned. These variations add to the overall aural impression, making Boogie-Woogie a unique and colorful piano style.

MELODY

Each jazz style treats the melodies associated with it in a unique manner, and Boogie-Woogie is no exception. The rhythmic drive of the bass in this style makes a rhythmic melody a necessity. The Boogie-Woogie melodic line in general is composed of short phrases, comparable to the riffs of other jazz styles, which are usually from two to four measures in length.

Syncopated chords are frequently played with orchestra voicing.

Example 15   Example 16

This melodic line is often made much more interesting by the use of sequential patterns and polyrhythms.

Example 17

Example 18

Phrases are often composed of tonal repetitions, short scalar sequences, and chromatic figures.

Example 19

Example 20

Example 21

Since the best Boogie-Woogie melodies are patterned after improvised solos, they must be alive and colorful in order to sound authentic. In other words, they must swing.

DEVICES AND SPECIAL EFFECTS

Many Boogie-Woogie pieces are played in the keys of C, F, and G, because in these and other related keys, the pianist is able to slide from the black keys to the white keys for certain effects.

Example 22

The sound of seconds, thirds, and fourths played simultaneously is familiar to everyone who has listened to Boogie-Woogie played by an expert.

Example 23

Example 24

Example 25

Some phrases are played in octaves to give better balance between the melody and the bass line.

Example 26

One of the most popular devices used by Boogie-Woogie pianists is the tremolo played with two hands.

Example 27

This device is used for introductions and interludes and is sometimes begun with an embellishment of one, two, or three grace notes.

Example 28

Sometimes a tremolo is played with a bass figure.

Example 29

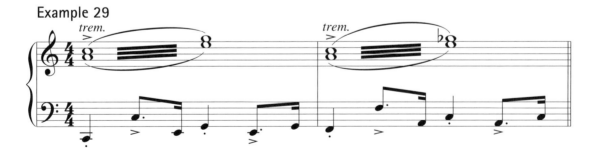

Boogie-Woogie pianists often use sustained chords in the left hand during the introduction or interlude so that the contrast will be greater when the bass figure starts.

Example 30

Sometimes instead of sustaining the chords, the pianist plays only single bass notes, on the beat, giving the effect of a "break," before the Boogie-Woogie left-hand part kicks in.

Example 31

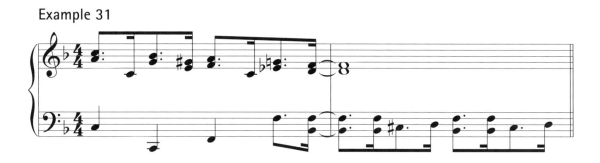

These effects play a big part in giving Boogie-Woogie a sound unlike any other style of jazz piano.

INDEPENDENCE OF HANDS

Boogie-Woogie must swing or it is not authentic. The Boogie-Woogie pianist must learn to project the beat while both hands are playing different rhythms. This means that the hands must be completely independent of each other.

The left hand must play the rhythmic figure solidly and must articulate the patterns in a crisp, clear fashion while laying a firm foundation for the right hand.

The right hand must give its syncopations their natural expression, unhampered by the impelling rhythm of the left hand, because the playing of one rhythm against another gives Boogie-Woogie the rhythmic drive which distinguishes it from other styles of jazz piano playing.

HOW TO ADD BOOGIE-WOOGIE BASS TO A POPULAR TUNE

Boogie-Woogie, like other jazz piano styles, is used in special arrangements of popular tunes. The addition of a Boogie-Woogie bass line does not necessarily make it a jazz interpretation, but in many cases it gives the tune a new rhythmic personality that adds new meaning to its syncopations. Here is a simplified version of "Camptown Races."

Example 32: De Camptown Races

by STEPHEN C. FOSTER

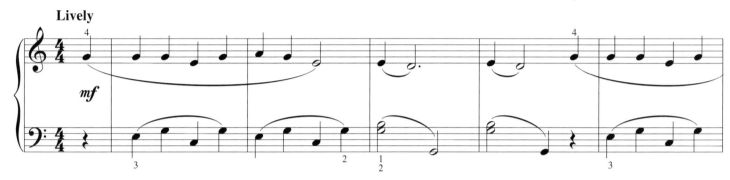

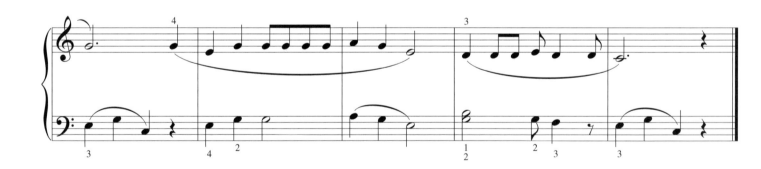

First, we experiment with a few bass patterns.

Example 33

Example 34

Example 35

Example 36

Next, we pick the one we think is the best suited for this piece and alter the melody to balance it with the bass line.

Example 37

When we are finished, "Camptown Races" sounds like this.

DE CAMPTOWN RACES
(Boogie-Woogie Version)

by STEPHEN C. FOSTER

SUGGESTIONS FOR PLAYING BOOGIE-WOOGIE SOLOS

Essential Points to Remember:

1. Boogie-Woogie is a "two-handed" style of piano playing, so pay careful attention to the syncopations in both hands.

2. Articulate the notes cleanly.

3. If at first you find it difficult to play both hands together, practice the bass alone. When you have mastered the bass, then add the treble.

4. Do not let the bass overshadow the treble. Strive for "balanced" playing.

5. Do not attempt to play too fast. Choose a comfortable tempo and stick to it until you make the whole piece swing.

6. Emphasize the polyrhythms and discordant effects, because often they are used to create tensions and add interest and color to the piece.

7. Listen to as many examples of authentic Boogie as possible and study the various tone shading used by those who play it best.

The above suggestions will aid you tremendously in the mastering and enjoyment of the four original Boogie-Woogie piano solos that appear on the following pages.

BEER BARREL BOOGIE

by BILLY TAYLOR

Not too fast

LUCKY BUCK BOOGIE

by BILLY TAYLOR

JELLY-BEAN BOOGIE

by BILLY TAYLOR

LET 'EM ROLL

by BILLY TAYLOR

DIXIELAND

WHAT IS DIXIELAND?

Dixieland originated in the southern part of America in the early 1900s, when white musicians began to try to play music in a style similar to that of the African-American jazz musicians of the period. A few of them managed to assimilate this interpretive style, but the majority merely took the African-American jazz repertory and played it in their own style. Because of their different backgrounds, both musical and hereditary, their interpretation of the African-American music resulted in something quite different. They retained some of its elements, modified others, and added many features of their own. Since many of them had studied music, they often substituted written music for improvised music and innovation, which made their music less flexible than the jazz music of the same period. All of this, together with their inclination to formalize the music they played, caused them finally to emerge with a definite style of playing which, though it also featured syncopation and some improvisation, was not jazz. It was a new way of playing music, not a new music.

After a while, Dixieland musicians and jazz musicians began to migrate to Chicago, where they enjoyed wide popularity and financial success. It was during this period of "cashing in on the craze" that Dixieland and jazz were first confused with one another. There was the Original Dixieland Jazz Band, whose very name added to the confusion, but which played a great part in popularizing this exciting style of playing. Another factor that contributed to misconceptions were the recordings on which jazz musicians played side by side with Dixieland musicians. To many listeners, these recordings brought out the similarities in their playing rather than the differences.

It is, of course, a fact that Dixieland has many characteristics that may also be found in jazz. However, jazz is a people's music—dynamic, varied, flexible, experimental, and constantly changing—while Dixieland is a style and a repertory based on this music. Dixieland is much narrower in concept, less varied in content, and almost inflexible in its performance. Yet it has been tremendously important to the development of jazz because its exponents created not only a demand for their music, but for jazz as well.

RHYTHM

One of the basic components of rhythm is pulse (or beat), the regular recurrence of time distances. This pulse is divided into units or measures (i.e., 2/4, 3/4, 4/4, etc.) by means of accent.

The vital principle of rhythm is the fact that though the beats are absolutely alike in duration, they differ in dynamic stress, some being strong and others weak. In the legitimate 4/4 beat the first beat is the strongest, the third beat is less strong, and the second and fourth beats are weak. In Dixieland, however, the second and fourth beats are also accented. This is the first step toward syncopation, Dixieland style.

When playing with groups, the Dixieland pianist is expected to play "rhythm," which means that he accents the first and third beats in the bass with his left hand and the second and fourth beats with his right. This method of playing the basic rhythmic and harmonic structures of a piece was also called "Boston Playing" and later, "comp."

The Dixieland beat, then, must always be felt as two accented beats in the course of four, and though it is definitely related to the legitimate 2/4 and 4/4 beats, it is fundamentally a syncopated beat, accenting the second and fourth beats in its own unique fashion.

MELODY

A melody is a series of single tones rhythmically arranged so as to produce a pleasing effect on the ear. Dixieland melodies are usually distinguished by brief syncopated phrases, from one to four measures in length, which are played with the feeling of the "Dixieland beat." Almost any melody can be played in this manner, but it must be remembered that some music is more adaptable to this style and therefore sounds better when transformed into "Dixieland" than other music. Because of the brevity and simplicity of many of the best "Dixieland" melodies, they are quite easy to sing.

HARMONY

The early Dixieland harmonies consisted mainly of basic chords.

Dissonance for the most part was accidental. In fact, in many of the early Dixieland pieces, the most dissonant chords were the diminished and the seventh chords.

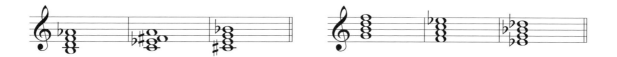

However, as Dixieland developed, pianists added more notes to their chords and soon chords like these were found.

HOW TO PLAY DIXIELAND

The Dixieland style of piano playing is identified by its beat and the "swing" of its melodic line. The first step in playing the piano with a Dixieland beat is to master playing the "Boston Style" (or "comp") with the left hand alone.

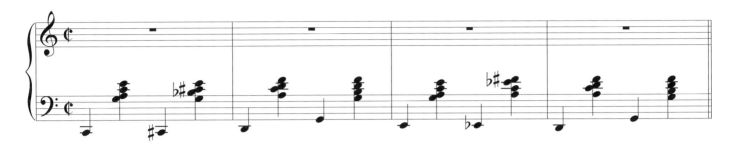

Make it sound like this:

When you have learned to control your left hand, add a melody. Be certain, however, that it is rhythmically accurate.

Remember, you must master *both* hands. Play the bass notes and the chords precisely, and do not let your beat be upset by the right hand rhythmic figures. Coordination is the key to this style of playing.

Dixieland piano is not an "off-beat" style of playing. Much of its syncopation stems from its basic beat and because of this it has a vitality comparable to the jazz beat, and like jazz it sometimes creates a unique excitement.

In attempting to maintain the Dixieland beat do not let the left hand dominate the right. Let it be steady without being forced, and let your playing be relaxed at all times. Do not attempt to play too fast; always play in a tempo that is comfortable.

The "Dixieland tag" is a codetta or short addition at the end of the composition. It may be from one to eight bars in length depending on the whim of the player. In many cases it has become a standard part of the piece.

There have been comparatively few changes in the Dixieland style of playing. However, some of the newer devices and techniques discovered by jazz musicians have been adapted. Some of the devices that should be mentioned are:

a. The use of tenths in the left hand.

b. The addition of passing notes to chords played in arpeggio form.

c. More complex harmonies.

d. More improvised solos.

Many contemporary Dixieland musicians sometimes employ these and other new devices, but the basic beat and character of Dixieland remains the same.

BIG SHOE SHUFFLE

by BILLY TAYLOR

SOCIETY STRUT

by BILLY TAYLOR

Allegretto

HOT PEPPER STOMP

by BILLY TAYLOR

Medium tempo

HOGHEAD SHOUT

by BILLY TAYLOR

Brightly

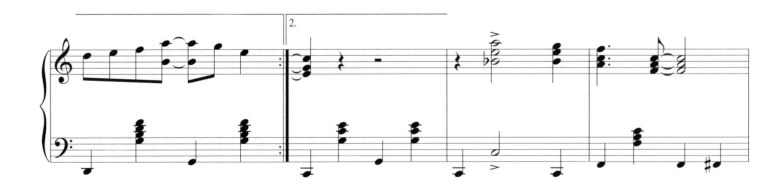

MAMBO

WHAT IS MAMBO?

Of all the Latin American music, the music of Cuba is perhaps the most popular the world over. This may be due to the fact that Cuban music was the first Latin American music to spread to North America and to Europe. From the Habanera of a century ago to the Rhumba, Bolero, Afro, Son, Guaracha, Conga, etc. of today, the music of Cuba has captured the fancy of the world.

However, Cuban popular music has undergone many changes and developments as a result of its contact with jazz, though the exciting and intricate rhythmic combinations have remained basically the same. Inspired by the "Montuno" (an ad lib. solo, alternately sung and played with the animated accompaniment of as many percussion instruments as possible), a popular Cuban contribution to Latin American music is the Mambo.

The Mambo was originally a part of the arrangement rather than a part of the song itself. Constructed by writing a rhythmic figure for the brass and a contrapuntal obbligato (usually in unison) for the saxes, the Mambo was often played between Montunos to add to the excitement of the arrangement. In other words, the Mambo was similar at first to a "shout" chorus played by a jazz band. This innovation became so popular that soon its infectious rhythms were applied to the entire piece, so that we now have the Mambo as a separate dance form.

Like the music of other Latin American countries, Cuban popular music is basically rhythmic, being a musical pattern of the rhythms of the various dance forms (Rhumba, Conga, Afro, etc.) with the melody added as an embellishment. However, Cuban instrumentalists, being accustomed to complex rhythms, are never puzzled when intricate combinations of rhythms are played simultaneously; rather they experiment and improvise and accent their rhythms exactly as they feel them. Since all authentic Cuban music conforms to the fundamental beat of the claves, the invigorating rhythmic variations enhance this basic beat and give the music its intensified vitality.

In developing a feeling for the Mambo, it often helps to listen to performances of the leading exponents of the style. Listen to the orchestras as well as the pianists, because the more familiar you are with the sound and rhythmic drive of the Mambo, the easier it is to play. There are many excellent examples of the correct way to play the Mambo to be found on recordings by Machito, Rene Hernandez, Perez Pardon, Miguelito Valdez, Marceline Guerra, Julio Anion, and Tito Rodriguez.

THE MAMBO BEAT

The Mambo, like all other Cuban music, is based on a two-measure rhythmic pattern called the "Clave." This rhythmic figure is usually played on the claves, a pair of round wooden sticks about one inch in diameter and eight inches in length. They are struck one against the other with the cupped palm of one hand serving as a resonator, and give forth a hollow but rather penetrating sound, thereby establishing a definite tempo and acting as a rhythmic guide to the other instruments.

Example 1

The Clave:

This two-measure rhythmic pattern is repeated in sequence throughout all Cuban pieces.

Example 2

Melody

Claves

etc.

However, it is frequently reversed. In such cases the piece begins with the second measure of the Clave and continues the pattern in this reversed manner until the end.

Example 3

Melody

Claves

etc.

The rhythmic structure of the melodic line determines the position of the Clave beat. A melody is "in Clave" when the beats of the Clave coincide with the accents in the melody. This may be true even when the rhythm of the melody differs from that of the clave.

Example 4

Melody

Claves

All Mambo rhythms, no matter how syncopated, must conform to the Clave, so it is obvious that the Clave beat must be thoroughly understood before one can play the Mambo authentically.

Example 5

MELODY

American jazz has had a tremendous influence on many Cuban musicians, and this influence is clearly shown in Mambo melodies. The infectious phrases of many of these melodies are quite jazz-like in conception and execution.

Example 6

The melody of the Mambo is dynamic, and when played by an expert it "swings" in a manner comparable to a jazz melody. Due to its orchestral origin, it suggests harmonies that are more modern than those used in much of the music that preceded it, and its intervals are better adapted for instrumental interpretation than vocal.

Example 7

Despite their jazz-like accents, authentic Mambo melodies are always "in Clave."

HARMONY

For many years Cuban musicians were so preoccupied with the development of their intricate and exciting rhythmic combinations that the harmonic side of their music remained virtually unchanged. They were content to use, for the most part, only the most basic chords.

Example 8   **Example 9**

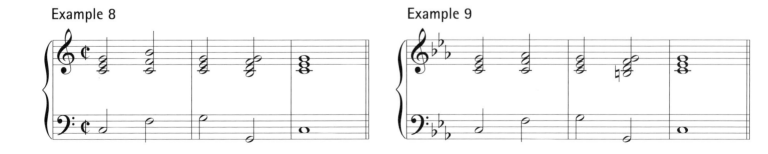

However, in recent years there has been a tendency to experiment more and more with the harmonic potential of Cuban music. Now with the emergence of the Mambo we find evidence of the incorporation of modern harmonic principles into the popular music of Cuba. In the Mambo one often hears chords like these:

Example 10

Example 11

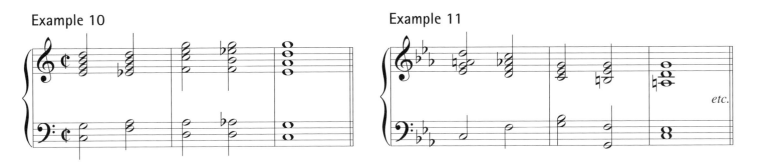

HOW TO PLAY THE MAMBO

The Mambo uses the rhythmic patterns of many other Cuban dance forms. Thus, we have Guaracha-Mambos, Son-Mambos, Afro-Mambos, and many other interesting combinations. All Mambos are basically orchestral pieces, but many may be adapted and arranged for piano.

When played by the solo pianist, the Mambo presents a unique problem. Not only must the pianist try to project its distinctive rhythmic drive, but he must also imitate or suggest the screaming brass and syncopated sax figures. This is usually done by alternating harmonized figures with melodic figures.

Example 12

Above all, the pianist must remember that despite the jazz influence the Mambo must be played "in Clave."

In the solos that follow, the bass figures are relatively simple because the solo pianist must compensate for the absence of percussion instruments by the use of a very definite and precisely played bass line.

PAN AMERICAN CLIPPER

by BILLY TAYLOR

Fine

1.

2.

D.S. al Fine

77

MAMBOLA

by BILLY TAYLOR

MAMBO MAGIC

by BILLY TAYLOR

OLD MAN MAMBO

by BILLY TAYLOR

Tickle the Ivories

with these great instruction books from Hal Leonard

ACCOMPANYING THE JAZZ/POP VOCALIST

A Practical Guide for Pianists

by Gene Rizzo

In this book/CD pack, author and pianist Gene Rizzo reveals the secrets to getting on a singer's accompanist "A" list, covering topics including: exploring song forms, intros and endings, writing a lead sheet, accompanying different vocal styles, descriptive accompaniment, tempo rubato, transposition and more. Appropriate for both solo piano accompanists and players who are part of a combo.

00290527 Book/CD Pack $14.95

AMAZING PHRASING

50 Ways to Improve Your Improvisational Skills

by Debbie Denke

Amazing Phrasing is for any keyboard player interested in learning how to improvise and how to improve their creative phrasing. You'll learn approaches to working with and around other musicians, and you'll practice comping and soloing over progressions in various styles – from rock to bossa nova to swing to bebop.

00842030 Book/CD Pack $16.95

INTROS, ENDINGS & TURNAROUNDS FOR KEYBOARD

Essential Phrases for Swing, Latin, Jazz Waltz, and Blues Styles

by John Valerio

Learn the intros, endings and turnarounds that all of the pros know and use! This book covers swing styles, ballads, Latin tunes, jazz waltzes, blues, major and minor keys, vamps and pedal tones, and more.

00290525 ....$12.95

JAZZ PIANO

An In-Depth Look at the Styles of the Masters

by Liam Noble

Featuring lessons, music, historical analysis and rare photos, this book/CD pack provides a complete overview of the techniques and styles popularized by 15 of the greatest jazz pianists of all time. All the best are here: from the early ragtime stylings of Ferdinand "Jelly Roll" Morton, to the modal escapades of Bill Evans, through the '70s jazz funk of Herbie Hancock.

00311050...$17.95

JAZZ PIANO VOICINGS

An Essential Resource for Aspiring Jazz Musicians

by Rob Mullins

The jazz idiom can often appear mysterious and difficult for musicians who were trained to play other types of music. Long-time performer and educator Rob Mullins helps players enter the jazz world by providing voicings that will help the player develop skills in the jazz genre. Includes a "Numeric Voicing Chart," chord indexes in all 12 keys, info about what range of the instrument you can play chords in, and a beginning approach to bass lines.

00310914 ....$19.95

KEYBOARD COOKBOOK

Recipes for Playing More Than 40 Styles

Spice up your playing today! This book provides the essential ingredients for 40 popular piano styles, including: bebop • bluegrass • classic rock • classical • contemporary R&B • cool jazz • Delta blues • early rock 'n' roll • folk • Motown • new age • ragtime • soul • stride • tango • and more. The CD includes demonstration tracks for all 40 styles, so you'll have a recipe for success!

00311009 Book/CD Pack $17.95

MODERN JAZZ PIANO

An Intermediate Guide to Jazz Concepts,

Improvisation, Technique & Theory

by Sarah Jane Cion

Learn the foundational concepts behind the wonderful world of jazz music. This book covers what every aspiring jazz pianist needs to know: jazz theory, harmony, rhythm, improvisation and more. The accompanying CD provides 15 full-band tracks to go along with the transcriptions inside the book.

00311144 Book/CD Pack $19.95

101 KEYBOARD TIPS

Stuff All the Pros Know and Use

by Craig Weldon

Ready to take your keyboard playing to the next level? This book will show you how. The text, photos, music, diagrams and accompanying CD provide an essential, easy-to-use resource for a variety of topics, including: techniques, improvising and soloing, equipment, practicing, ear training, performance, theory, and much more.

00310933 Book/CD Pack $14.95

THE PROFESSIONAL SOLO PIANIST

Techniques for the Self-Contained

Performance of Jazz and Popular Music

by Gene Rizzo

Learn the tricks of the trade with this complete resource for performing solo in any style: cocktail, stride, jazz, Latin-American, rock, pop, and more! Essential for every pianist.

00294031 ....$12.95

TEACH YOURSELF TO PLAY PIANO

A Quick and Easy Introduction for Beginners

This easy-to-understand book will get you playing right away and at your own pace, in the comfort of your home! Learn everything from hand position and good posture to playing melodies and songs. By the end of the book, you'll be able to play hands together, using a combination of whole, half, quarter and eighth notes and their respective rests. You will also be able to read a selection of notes from both the bass and treble clefs, and you will be able to play some simple chords in the left hand.

00311085 Piano Instruction.........................$5.95

Prices and availability subject to change without notice.

FOR MORE INFORMATION, SEE YOUR LOCAL MUSIC DEALER,
OR WRITE TO:

HAL•LEONARD® CORPORATION

7777 W. BLUEMOUND RD. P.O. BOX 13819 MILWAUKEE, WI 53213

Visit Hal Leonard Online at
www.halleonard.com

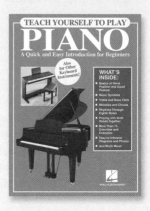

JAZZ PIANO

from **ABRSM PUBLISHING**

in Association with Hal Leonard Corporation

Jazz Piano **LEVEL 1**

The Complete Method
- based on the world-famous ABRSM assessment program
- 15 pieces, including well-known jazz standards
- aural tests and quick studies
- scales and arpeggios

CD INCLUDED

HAL•LEONARD
ABRSM PUBLISHING

"What good is music if it ain't got that swing?"

— Duke Ellington

The Associated Board responds with *Jazz Piano*, a comprehensive introduction to the world of jazz. A pioneering set of publications and optional assessment materials provide the building blocks you need to play jazz with imagination, understanding, and style, and to improvise effectively right from the start. Five levels of graded pieces contain a wide range of styles: funky jazz, up-tempo swing, calypso, Latin, jazz waltz, modal, bebop, Gospel, ragtime, free jazz, and more. There are classic tunes by Duke Ellington, Miles Davis, Bill Evans, and Thelonious Monk. Within each level there are 15 pieces, aural tests, quick studies, scales, arpeggios, and a CD with play-along tracks. The 15 pieces are presented in three categories: blues, standards, and contemporary jazz. Each piece provides a head/melody which contains all the characteristic voicings, phrasing, and rhythmic patterns needed for a stylish performance. An improvised section follows, where guideline pitches and left-hand voicings are given as a practical starting point for solos. Totally accessible and at the highest musical standards, these pieces provide the opportunity to play jazz confidently and creatively.

JAZZ PIANO – LEVEL 1

Level 1 includes: Bags' Groove • Bedford Square Blues • Blue Autumn • Bottle Junction • He Is Sadly Melting • Here We Go Again • The Inch Worm • Is You Is, or Is You Ain't (Ma' Baby) • Jean Pierre • O, Lord, Please Don't Let Them Drop That Atomic Bomb on Me • (Old Man From) The Old Country • Perdido • Prove You Groove • Slinky Thing • Yokate.

_____00290529 Book/CD Pack.............$12.95

JAZZ PIANO – LEVEL 2

Level 2 includes: Becky's Song • Big Noise from Winnetka • Blue Lullaby • C-Jam Blues • Contemplation • The Firefly • Good Time Blues • Hard Science • Moanin' • Now's the Time • On-Off Boogie • The Orchard • Softly as in a Morning Sunrise • St. Thomas • Swing It and C.

_____00290530 Book/CD Pack............$12.95

JAZZ PIANO – LEVEL 3

Level 3 includes: Allfarthing Blues • Barrelhouse Blues • Birk's Works • Blues for Tom • Fly Me to the Moon (In Other Words) • I Wish I Knew How It Would Feel to Be Free • Neat Feet • The Peanut Vendor (El Manisero) • Sails • Saturday • A Smooth One • Sombrero Sam • Spanish Sketch • Swing Fun • Walking Blues.

_____00290531 Book/CD Pack...........$12.95

Prices, contents, and availability subject to change without notice.

FOR MORE INFORMATION, SEE YOUR LOCAL MUSIC DEALER, OR WRITE TO:

HAL•LEONARD® CORPORATION

7777 W. BLUEMOUND RD. P.O. BOX 13819 MILWAUKEE, WI 53213

Visit Hal Leonard Online at
www.halleonard.com

JAZZ PIANO – LEVEL 4

Level 4 includes: Blue Monk • Blues for Pe Johnson • Footprints • Freddie Freeloader Heading Home • I'm Beginning to See the Light Ikon (Memories of Ike) • In a Different Light • La River • Nobody Knows the Trouble I've Seen Original Rags • Oscar's Boogaloo • Shh! • Thre Four Blues • Undecided.

_____00290532 Book/CD Pack...........$12.9

JAZZ PIANO – LEVEL 5

Level 5 includes: All Blues • Blue Bossa • Chop • Christopher Columbus • Crossover Blues Jamming with Jools • Lemon Cornette • Mamb Country • Oleo • An Oscar for Oscar • So Long Take the "A" Train • That Monday Morning Feelin • Waltz for Autumn • 34 Skidoo.

_____00290533 Book/CD Pack...........$12.9

JAZZ PIANO FROM SCRATCH

Jazz Piano from Scratch is a complete step-by-step guide to playing jazz with confidence and style. Designed for the absolute beginner, it breaks down the process into simple yet fun activities, with many musical examples to illustrate the points made. The accompanying CD provides examples, activities, and some great trio playing to use as a backdrop to the student's own work. Together with a range of other supporting materials – pieces, scales, quick studies, aural tests and CDs – this book provides a comprehensive introduction to the world of jazz.

_____00290534 Book/CD Pack $24.95

110